QUICK POPS™

Fast & delicious recipes from the pop-crazy
creators of the Zoku™ Quick Pop™ Maker

Jackie Zorovich   **ZOKU**™   Kristina Sacci

Library of Congress Cataloging–in–Publication
data is available.

Published by Zoku, LLC
720 Monroe Street, Suite C405
Hoboken, NJ 07030
www.zokuhome.com

ISBN: 978-0-615-39120-5

First Printing 2010

10 9 8 7 6 5 4 3 2 1

Printed in China

CREATED & PRODUCED
Zoku, LLC

BOOK DESIGNER
Kristina Sacci

PHOTOGRAPHER
Yos Kumthampinij

**PHOTO RETOUCHING
& COLOR CORRECTION**
Monica Collins

FOOD STYLISTS
Jackie Zorovich
Kristina Sacci
Ken Zorovich

PROP STYLISTS
Yos Kumthampinij
Ken Zorovich

ART DIRECTOR
Ken Zorovich

Thanks!

We would like to thank our families and friends for all of their encouragement and for tasting countless pops with us!

Extra Thanks

QUICK POP™ TASTERS
Patrick Filler
Our friends at Harvest
Pamela Huggins
Teri Thompson
Kesha Alexander
Marni Landes

PHOTOGRAPHY ASSISTANT
Alaina Sacci

FRIENDS & ADVISORS
Carol Durst-Wertheim, Ph.D. and
Trish Lobenfeld, CCP, who we met at
the Stone Barns Writing Food Memoir workshop,
Shawn Askinosie, and Craig Wallace Dale

Last but not least, special thanks
to all of the Zoku fans around the world
who have inspired us to create this book.

Table of Contents

About

Tips

Techniques

Etc.

Fresh & Fruity

I Scream for Quick Pops!™

Bake Shop

Coco Loco

Making the Quick Pop™ Maker

Zoku is a design collective dedicated to making innovative products. We noticed that the process of making ice pops at home hadn't changed since the first pop molds were invented back in the early 1900s. Almost every technology that we could think of has seen profound improvements (especially in speed) over the past 100 years. So why was it that the process for making ice pops hadn't changed at all?

We asked a simple question: could we make pops *faster*?

To find out if it was possible, we brought together our design and engineering teams to brainstorm ideas. We began building multitudes of prototypes to test our different theories. After many months of experimenting, we started to get results. We could actually make pops fast with our new invention! Our early prototypes weren't pretty, but they worked and gave us the confidence to move forward. As we tested our prototypes, we discovered that creating ice pops instantly with our new device was a fun and magical experience. Every time we made a pop, it brought a smile to our faces, and to the faces of everyone who tried it, regardless of their age.

Once we mastered the technology to make ice pops quickly, we started to experiment with various pop–making techniques using our new "Quick Pop" maker. We made striped pops and then tried making different flavored core pops by extracting the unfrozen liquid from the inside of a pop and filling it with a second flavor. We also tried applying fruit slices to the walls of the molds to decorate them. We soon discovered that not only could we make ice pops quickly with our new Quick Pop Maker, but we could also make beautiful pops that were previously impossible or really time–consuming to make at home. The few minutes spent waiting for our pops to freeze gave us a little quality time with our families while making healthy treats.

We hope that these recipes will bring you many smiles. Happy Quick Popping!
– The Zoku Team

Want More?

Check out our blog at **blog.zokuhome.com** and follow us on Twitter for even more Zoku news, recipes & tips.

Making the Book

As soon as Zoku launched the Quick Pop Maker, they were inundated with e-mails from enthusiastic customers asking for recipes. Eager to satisfy the need of its loyal fans, Zoku presented us with the opportunity to put together this comprehensive collection of delicious recipes that takes advantage of the unique properties of the Quick Pop Maker.

We developed this book with the same level of energy and zeal that the Zoku team applied while creating the Quick Pop Maker. We spent countless hours experimenting with the flavor profiles and techniques that are presented on the pages before you.

With our tips and recipes you'll easily master fun techniques while making the most delicious pops you've ever tasted! **– Jackie & Kristina**

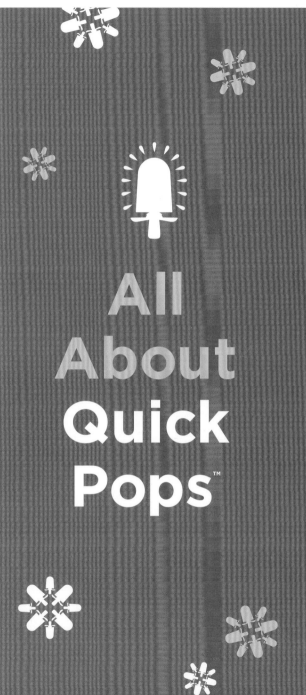

All About Quick Pops™

Zoku™ Tools & Accessories

*"The Super what?" If you're confused about all of the tools that make the Quick Pop Maker extra awesome, here's a handy guide that will explain everything. Zoku tools & replacement parts can be purchased at **zokuhome.com**.*

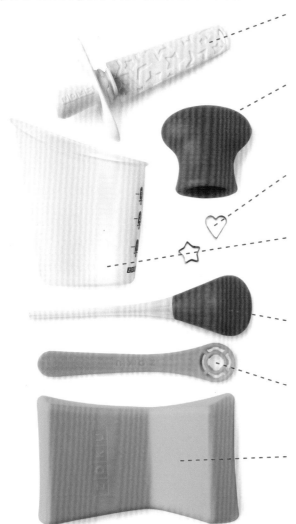

POP STICKS & DRIP CUPS Our durable, reusable pop sticks come with special drip guards for tidy eating.

THE SUPER TOOL Once frozen, pops are locked into the ice-cold pop maker. Only the Super Tool has the super strength to remove them quickly and with ease.

FRUIT STENCILS Easily cut perfect hearts and stars with our stencils to make fun decorated pops! See technique, p. 24.

POUR CUP Measure your pop mixture using the lines on the side of the pour cup. Lean the front of the cup on the edge of the pop maker for a neater pour.

SIPHON Make flavored core pops (see opposite page) and easily fill tilted molds when using the angle tray.

FRUIT WAND Apply fruit slices and cut-outs to the walls of the pop maker molds. See technique, p. 24.

ANGLE TRAY Make insane angled pops in minutes. See technique, p. 21.

STORAGE CASE Store Quick Pops, protect them from freezer burn, and create a beautiful presentation at the table. Photo, p. 30.

Quick Pop™ Anatomy

Here's a helpful breakdown of the unique components of a Quick Pop. Don't sweat it though, there won't be a pop quiz following this anatomy lesson!

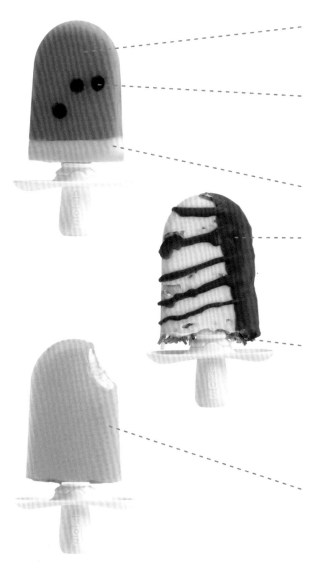

POP MIXTURE / POP BASE The liquid (store-bought or homemade) part of the pop recipe.

EXTRAS Add extras like chocolate chips and chopped cookies pre-freeze or post-freeze. For a list of tasty extras and tips for applying them, see p. 23.

LAYERS Pop layers can be straight, wavy, marbled or angled. For more info, see p. 20.

QUICK SHELLS Watching chocolate freeze instantly over your pop will make your heart go *pitter-patter*. Not to mention, the shells add extra flavor. See tips, p. 28 and recipes, p. 29.

SKIRT After pouring a thick pop base (for example, yogurt) into the pop maker molds, you can top it with extras without having them sink into the molds. The decorated edge (skirt) will add a little flair and flavor to the bottom of your pop. See examples, p. 73 and p. 78.

CORE POP A pop with an outer layer that envelops an inner core layer. See technique, p. 25 and recipes, p. 27.

General Tips

*Here are some tips to ensure successful Quick Popping! For even more tips and tricks from Zoku, visit our blog at **blog.zokuhome.com**.*

START WITH CHILLED INGREDIENTS
so that your pops will freeze as quickly as possible. If you start with room temperature ingredients, your pops will take an extra few minutes to freeze.

SET THE TEMPERATURE OF YOUR FREEZER at or below 0°F (–18°C), which is also the ideal temperature for food storage.

LEAVE YOUR POP MAKER IN THE FREEZER 24/7 so that it will be ready to make tasty pops anytime!

YOUR POPS MAY TAKE LONGER TO FREEZE if your pop mixture has a high fat or solids content. Pops made with juice have a lower fat content and therefore freeze faster.

USE PRECISE MEASUREMENTS when following these recipes to ensure that you end up with the right volume and flavor. The small volume of these recipes makes accurate measurement very important, so be sure to level your tablespoons and cups when measuring ingredients. For best results, we recommend weighing produce on a kitchen scale as opposed to using a measuring cup.

REFRIGERATE YOUR POP MIXTURES
to speed the cooling process after preparing recipes that require ingredients to be heated.

STIR YOUR POP MIXTURES in between batches because they may separate slightly when left to settle. Also, store your mixtures in the refrigerator in between batches to ensure they're chilled for your next batch.

DO NOT FILL PAST THE FILL LINE
to ensure that the Super Tool can remove your pops. See your Quick Pop Maker Instruction Manual for more details.

FREEZE YOUR POPS USING THE ZOKU QUICK POP MAKER when following our recipes, which rely on the ability to freeze pops in just minutes. Why would you want to wait hours for pops anyway?

STORE POPS IN THE ZOKU STORAGE CASE (shown on p. 30) to keep pops fresh and to prevent freezer burn.

Additional Tools

The Zoku Tools (p. 12) make gorgeous pops, but there are still a few fundamental kitchen tools that will help make your pop-making sessions a breeze.

WHISK & BLENDER Thoroughly combine or puree ingredients.

CHEESE CLOTH Strain out solids that may prevent pops from freezing.

CHOPSTICK Test if pops are fully frozen. Also, use the blunt end to pack down crumbled cookies into a dense layer.

FOOD PROCESSOR Crush cookies & nuts with the convenient push of a button.

HEADLAMP OR FLASHLIGHT Light the inside of pop molds when intricately decorating them or using the Zoku Angle Tray.

JUICER Extract juice from mangoes, carrots and other fresh produce.

MESH SIEVE Strain seeds out of fruit blends for a smooth consistency.

KITCHEN SCALE Weigh your ingredients for accuracy.

TWEEZERS Easily apply chocolate chips and other extras to the walls of the molds.

Beyond the Book

Feeling adventurous? Here are some ways you can mix up our recipes or create some of your own.

FIRST THINGS FIRST, don't buy too much stuff. Each pop mold holds only about two ounces of liquid, so you don't need a lot to make multiple batches of pops.

CERTAIN INGREDIENTS may not work well in the Quick Pop Maker. Check out our lists of ingredients (p. 16) and extras (p. 23) to see what works best.

TASTE what you've prepared before freezing your pops. It always helps to make pop mixtures a little extra flavorful (e.g. with more sugar or vanilla extract) since certain flavors can lose a little of their oomph once frozen.

RE-MIX Layer stripes of different thicknesses, mix up the order of layers, or use the Zoku Angle Tray (p. 12) to create fun, geometric shapes. You can pick and choose elements from our recipes, make your own, or try different store-bought fruit juices and nectars. You can also experiment with different extras (p. 22) and Quick Shells (p. 28). Be creative!

Ingredients

For the ultimate pop experience, it's important to start with high-quality, great-tasting ingredients. One of the many benefits of making pops with the Zoku Quick Pop Maker is that you can control what goes into your pops instead of settling for store-bought pops that may contain artificial or low-quality ingredients. Also, since pops made with the Quick Pop Maker are ready in just minutes, you're tasting those wonderful ingredients at the peak of freshness.

Certain ingredients require a little extra care when used with the Quick Pop Maker. We are sharing our tips for using these ingredients so that every one of your pop-making sessions ends with you smiling, pop in hand!

Ingredients with high fat content and/or very low freezing points (see list below) should be used in moderation. When used in excess, these ingredients will produce pops that are too soft to pull out of the Quick Pop Maker– the pop stick will pull out from the mold without your pop attached! We have dubbed this preventable mishap a "soft pull."

Use ingredients so **fresh**, they're ready for their close-ups!

AVOID "SOFT PULLS" BY USING THE FOLLOWING IN MODERATION:

Alcohol

Butter

Buttermilk

Coconut milk

Cream cheese

Half & half

Heavy cream

Ice cream

Nut butters

Sour cream

Sweetened condensed milk

Fruit

Naturally sweet and jam-packed with vitamins, fruit makes great, healthy pops.

FRESH FRUIT Take advantage of local, seasonal fresh fruit whenever possible to maximize the flavor of your pops. You can blend or juice it to make pop mixtures or cut it into slices to decorate your pops (see technique, p. 24).

BOTTLED, FROZEN & CANNED These readily available alternatives to fresh fruit are great for satisfying those out-of-season fruit cravings.

Dairy & Non-Dairy

MILK Many of the recipes in this book call for whole milk to yield a creamier pop. If desired, you can always substitute lowfat milk; your pops will just be a little more firm and icy.

CREAM Just a touch of half & half or heavy cream can give your pops a creamier texture than milk, but use them in moderation to avoid the aforementioned "soft pull."

YOGURT & PUDDING Both of these ingredients will add a creamier, thicker texture to your pops. Dilute them with lowfat milk for easier pouring. Yogurt works best in recipes that are complemented by its characteristically tangy flavor.

BUTTERMILK, CREAM CHEESE & SOUR CREAM Like yogurt, these ingredients add a nice tang and thick texture to pops, but they do not freeze quite as well. Bring cream cheese to room temperature for easy mixing.

SWEETENED CONDENSED MILK This thick, canned milk lends a buttery flavor and creamy texture to pops.

DAIRY ALTERNATIVES Soy milk, rice milk, and vegan pudding all freeze well and can be substituted for cow's milk products.

ICE CREAM & FROZEN YOGURT Melted frozen yogurt and ice cream are not recommended for use with the Quick Pop Maker because they will yield a "soft pull." Instead, use other, better-freezing dairy products listed here and add your favorite extras and flavorings. Our Mint Chip Pop recipe (p. 61) is a good example of this method.

The Sweet Stuff

Generally speaking, it's probably safe to replace sweeteners in our recipes with one of your own preference. However, keep in mind that certain sweeteners like honey and agave have distinct flavors that may not agree with certain other flavors in your pop.

AGAVE NECTAR Pronounced "ah-GAH-vay", it's a natural sweetener made from the agave plant that comes in light and dark varieties. Since it's sweeter than sugar and honey, you'll want to use a bit less of it when making substitutions.

HONEY The flavor and aroma of this drizzly sweetener depends upon the bees' nectar source (for example: clover, orange blossoms, and wildflowers). Because it's so sticky, adding too much honey may result in a soft or sticky pull.

SUGAR We call for honey and agave in our recipes whenever these ingredients pair well with the flavors in the pop, but in some cases, the neutral flavor of sugar works best. **BROWN SUGAR** adds more of a caramel flavor than regular sugar.

ARTIFICIAL SWEETENERS & BEVERAGES
In our experiments, sugar–free products made with artificial sweeteners such as Splenda® may prevent pops from releasing from the molds. Artificial sweeteners can be combined with small amounts of natural fruit juices, honey, agave, or sugar, which will help the pops release from the molds while minimizing the overall sugar content.

SODA Let sodas go flat before freezing them. This will eliminate pockets of air (bubbles) from your pops, resulting in a smoother texture and better taste. If the soda is not flat, it may expand and overflow past the fill line, preventing the Super Tool from removing your pops.

CANDY You can drop candy into the molds as you pour your pop mixture– just make sure your candies are relatively small or chopped (1/4" x 1/4" or less) so that they can fit in the molds, past the pop sticks. Alternatively, you can wait until after you pull your frozen pop from the mold and use our Quick Shells (p. 28) to "glue" candy to the outside of the pop. Use candies that are easy to bite into, like malted milk balls– not jawbreakers!

COOKIES, PRETZELS & GRAHAM CRACKERS, OH MY! To prevent these crunchy treats from getting soggy, use a thick pop mixture (see Strawberry Short-pop, p. 71) so they won't absorb liquid as easily. Also, try crushing and packing them into a dense layer (see Pie Pops, p. 66).

Chocolate

Is high-quality chocolate more expensive than the average stuff? Yep. Is it worth the small investment? Absolutely! If you value yourself a true chocoholic, do your taste buds justice and demand only the finest.

MILK VS. DARK Milk chocolate contains sweeteners and milk and has a low percentage of cocoa liquor. Dark chocolate is less sweet, does not contain milk, and has a higher percentage of cocoa liquor. Dark chocolate takes longer to melt than milk chocolate, which is why we recommend using a clean spoon to check that no specks of unmelted chocolate remain in the pop mixture (for example, see our Oh, Fudge! Pop, p. 82).

Other Goodies

NUT BUTTERS Nut oils have low freezing points and since nut butters contain both natural and added oils, they do not freeze very well. They can be used in moderation if mixed with other fast-freezing ingredients.

NUTS You can incorporate nuts into pop mixtures by blending them with milk or water and then straining with a cheese cloth. This will preserve the nutty flavor while removing nut pieces and excessive oils, allowing the pops to freeze faster.

ALCOHOL "Can you make BEER pops?!" This is one of the first questions adults ask us when we tell them about the Quick Pop Maker. Yes, you can, but there are a few "rules" you'll need to keep in mind. Basically, the higher the alcohol content, the lower the freezing point and the more trouble you will have trying to make a pop. Beer has less alcohol and a higher freezing point than hard liquor, so it will freeze (though you'll want to let it go flat first– see **SODA**, p. 18). Hard liquors will not freeze in the pop maker unless you dilute them a lot with water or juice. You can also soak berries or flambé banana slices in liqueurs and add them to a non–alcoholic pop mixture.

Layers of Love

They say that magicians should never reveal their secrets. Good thing we're not magicians! Try these easy techniques and – presto! – you'll have impressive layered pops in minutes.

STRAIGHT EDGE For neat layers, lean your pour cup right on the rim of the pop maker; this balance will help you achieve a clean, dripless pour. Do not move the pop maker while layers are freezing and wait for each layer to freeze completely before adding the next one. Try this technique with our Pining for Papaya Pop (p. 48).

MARBLING This technique works best when you use two thick pop mixtures. You can pour both mixtures simultaneously or quickly rotate pouring them without letting them freeze completely so that they intertwine. Try this technique with our Strawberry Shortpop (p. 71).

MAKING ANGLES Making all sorts of crazy angles is easy when using the Zoku Angle Tray (p. 12). Experiment with setting the pop maker on the tray in various directions to make fun, geometric designs. If you set it at a sharp angle that makes it hard to use a pour cup, try using the Zoku Siphon (p. 12) to inject the pop mixture into the molds. Try this technique with our Black Raspberry Zig Zag Pop (p. 43).

MAKING WAVES As with marbling, this technique works best with thicker pop mixtures. Simply pour your first layer and immediately tilt the pop maker at an angle, holding it that way for about a minute. Gently set it down flat and let freeze completely. Repeat layering and tilting as desired until you reach the fill line. Try this technique with our Strawberry Banana Pop (p. 38).

Extras

Want to add a healthy crunch to your pop with some granola? How about some chopped pieces of your favorite candy bar? We fully encourage you to be creative and these tips will help you personalize your pops, whether you start with our recipes or your own.

LEFT This layered pop made with store-bought juices was decorated using the Zoku Fruit Wand (see technique, p. 24).

RIGHT Our Summer Morning Pop (p. 37) is garnished with sanding sugar to give it a little extra sweetness and pizazz.

Tips & Tricks

DIP FRUIT SLICES, CHOCOLATE CHIPS AND COOKIES in the pop mixture or brush them with honey before applying them to the walls of the pop maker molds so that they stick in place better.

EXTRAS SHOULD BE SMALL (1/4" x 1/4" or less) so they fit past the sticks and so that the pop mixture can sneak past them and fill the pop maker molds completely.

THICKER POP MIXTURES WORK BETTER with certain extras like cookies, which can get soggy if paired with a thin pop mixture. If the pop mixture is thick, extras won't be able to absorb it as easily as they would a thin mixture. Also, you can drop extras into a thick pop mixture as you pour without having them sink to the bottom of the molds.

IF YOUR POP MIXTURE IS THIN and extras sink to the bottom, simply apply extras to the walls of the pop maker molds using the dipping technique above.

QUICK SHELLS CAN BE USED TO "GLUE" EXTRAS TO FROZEN POPS Sometimes extras taste better and look prettier on the outside of a Quick Pop than they do on the inside. See Tartufo Pop (p. 57).

TO ENSURE POP STICKS ARE PROPERLY POSITIONED in the molds, insert the sticks and pour a drop of the pop mixture. The mixture will freeze almost instantly, securing the tip of the stick in place before you drop in your extras.

ASSEMBLE ONE POP AT A TIME when making certain pops like Strawberry Short-pop (p. 71) and Chocolate Coconut Cookie Mayhem (p. 79) so that you can drop in extras as you pour without the pop mixture freezing before you're done.

HERE'S A LIST TO GET YOU STARTED!
For more tips, check out the Ingredients section, p. 16.

- Sprinkles
- Sanding sugar
- Marshmallows
- Chocolate chips
- Cake & brownie pieces
- Fudge pieces
- Fruit slices & cutouts
- Maraschino cherries
- Crumbled cookies
- Chopped candy bars
- Chocolate–covered pretzels
- Nuts
- Cereal
- Granola
- Coconut flakes

How to Add Fruit Slices

Use the Zoku Fruit Stencils to cut out perfect hearts and stars that you can use to decorate pops! This technique works best with firm fruits like apples and pears.

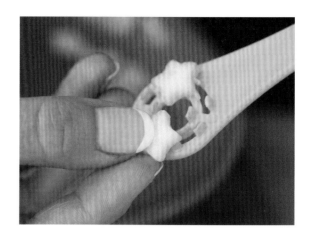

1 **SLICE FRUIT** 1/8" thick or less. Lay fruit slices flat on your cutting board and cut them with the fruit stencils. To keep the fruit cutouts from browning, transfer them to a bowl filled with a mix of water and a splash of lemon juice.

2 **ATTACH A FRUIT SLICE OR CUTOUT** to the end of the fruit wand. Before inserting the pop stick, insert the prepared fruit wand into the empty pop maker mold, pressing the fruit against the wall of the mold. The fruit will freeze to the mold almost instantly. Carefully detach the fruit wand and then use the flat side of the wand to press the fruit securely against the wall of the mold.

3 **INSERT THE POP STICK** and fill the mold with the pop mixture until you reach the fill line. Let freeze completely, then remove the pop with the Super Tool and enjoy!

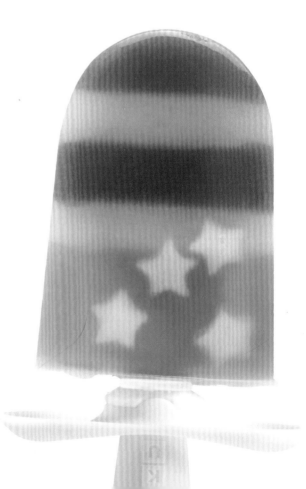

How to Make a Core Pop

When it comes to eating an ice pop, it doesn't get any better than biting into a seemingly plain jane pop to be surprised by a second flavor on the inside! The extremely fast freezing power of the Quick Pop Maker finally makes it possible to create this frozen masterpiece at home.

1 **INSERT THE POP STICK** into the pop maker mold and pour your outer layer up to the fill line. Wait until you see the outer edge freeze (30 seconds – 2 minutes). The longer you wait, the thicker the outer layer will be.

2 **EXTRACT THE UNFROZEN LIQUID** from the center of the mold by squeezing the bulb of the siphon, inserting the tip of the siphon into the liquid, and releasing the bulb to create suction. Alternatively, you can use a straw to suck the liquid out.

3 **POUR THE CORE FLAVOR** into the prepared mold. Let freeze completely then remove pop with the Super Tool and enjoy!

For tasty core pop recipes, see page 27.

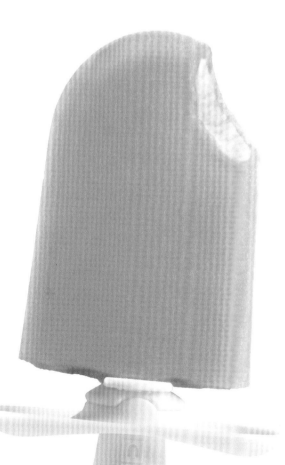

Core Pops
See How to Make a Core Pop, p. 25.

PURPLE OUTER LAYER
- 1 1/2 cups (7 1/2 oz) blackberries
- 1 1/2 cups (7 1/2 oz) blueberries
- 1/4 cup + 2 Tbsp (3 oz) half & half
- 1 1/2 Tbsp fresh lemon juice
- 2 1/2 Tbsp sugar
- 3/4 tsp vanilla extract

PINK OUTER LAYER
- 1 1/2 cups (8 1/2 oz) hulled, quartered strawberries
- 3 1/2 Tbsp whole milk
- 1/4 cup + 1 Tbsp (2 1/2 oz) heavy cream
- 3 Tbsp sugar
- 1 Tbsp vanilla extract

ORANGE OUTER LAYER
- 1 1/2 cups (9 oz) peeled, diced peaches (from about 1–2 peaches)
- 1/2 cup (4 oz) pure orange juice
- 1 Tbsp sweetened condensed milk
- 1 1/2 tsp agave nectar
- 3/4 tsp fresh lemon juice
- 1/4 + 1/8 tsp vanilla extract

VANILLA CORE LAYER
- 4 oz vanilla pudding (1 individual serving)
- 1/4 cup (2 oz) half & half
- 1/4 cup (2 oz) 2% milk
- 1 Tbsp + 1 tsp sweetened condensed milk
- 2 tsp sugar
- 1 1/2 tsp fresh lemon juice
- 1/2 tsp vanilla extract

MAKE THE PURPLE OUTER LAYER
Add berries and half & half to a blender and puree until smooth. Using a fine mesh sieve, strain the mixture into a medium bowl (using a spoon to scrape the sieve so it goes through faster). Add the lemon juice, sugar, and vanilla; whisk until incorporated and sugar has dissolved.

MAKE THE PINK OUTER LAYER Add strawberries and milk to a blender and puree until smooth. Using a fine mesh sieve, strain the mixture into a medium bowl (using a spoon to scrape the sieve so it goes through faster). Add the cream, sugar, and vanilla; whisk until incorporated and sugar has dissolved.

MAKE THE ORANGE OUTER LAYER
Combine the orange layer ingredients in a blender and puree until smooth.

MAKE THE VANILLA CORE LAYER
Whisk together the vanilla layer ingredients until sugar has dissolved.

ASSEMBLE THE POPS For assembly instructions, see p. 25. Each recipe yields 6 pops.

Pop Tip
Since you're siphoning off half of the outer layer, you'll have extra left over after making these recipes. Use it to make more pops– woohoo!

Quick Shells

Need a little something extra? Our Quick Shells will add another layer of deliciousness to any pop and the best part is: they freeze in seconds! We recommend using a double boiler to slowly melt the chocolate over indirect heat, preventing it from getting too hot and clumping or burning.

HOW TO MAKE A DOUBLE BOILER Place a non-reactive bowl over a small pot that's filled with an inch of barely simmering water. Do not let the bottom of the bowl touch the water.

WHAT TO DO WITH THE QUICK SHELLS
- Dip pops in them
- Pour or drizzle them over pops
- Use to "glue" candies or nuts to pops
- Add them as a layer right in the pop maker (just not as the first layer)

HOW TO STORE Pour Quick Shell into airtight, microwave-safe container; store in the refrigerator for up to three weeks. Quick Shell will harden when cold, so follow reheating instructions below.

HOW TO REHEAT Heat open container of Quick Shell in the microwave in short increments at half power or sit the closed container in a bath of hot water for a few minutes.

Chocolate Quick Shell

INGREDIENTS
- $2/3$ cup (4 oz) semi–sweet chocolate chips
- $1/3$ cup (2 $1/2$ oz) refined coconut oil

MAKE THE CHOCOLATE QUICK SHELL
In a double boiler over barely simmering water, whisk together the chocolate and coconut oil until the chocolate has completely melted. Remove from heat and let cool completely before applying to pops. Yields $3/4$ cup.

WHITE CHOCOLATE VARIATION
Substitute the semi–sweet chips with white chocolate chips.

TASTES GREAT ON
Mint Chip Pop, p. 61
Chocolate Coconut Cookie Mayhem, p. 79
Strawberry Banana, p. 38

Pop Tip
Coconut oil, made from the meat of the coconut, is solid at 76°F. This ingredient allows Quick Shells to harden when you pour them onto pops.

Peanut Butter Quick Shell

INGREDIENTS
- $1/3$ cup smooth peanut butter
- $1/3$ cup (2 $1/2$ oz) refined coconut oil

MAKE THE PEANUT BUTTER QUICK SHELL
Follow instructions for Chocolate Quick Shell (left). Yields $2/3$ cup.

TASTES GREAT ON
Vanilla Base, p. 57
Oh, Fudge! Pop, p. 82

Butterscotch Quick Shell

INGREDIENTS
- $1/2$ cup (3 oz) butterscotch chips
- $1/2$ cup (4 oz) refined coconut oil

MAKE THE BUTTERSCOTCH QUICK SHELL
Follow instructions for Chocolate Quick Shell (left). Yields $3/4$ cup.

TASTES GREAT ON
That's a S'more Pop, p. 83
The Banana Stand Pop, p. 88

Quick Pop™ Storage

Our pops are usually gobbled up within seconds of being removed from the pop maker, but every now and again you may have leftovers or you may want to make pops in advance for a party. In order to keep your pops protected from freezer burn and from getting tossed around in the freezer, the Zoku team created a convenient airtight storage case that holds up to six pops. You can also remove the cover for a great way to display and serve pops at the table. Your pops will look beautiful and taste even better, safe and sound in our special case.

*To purchase the Zoku Storage Case and other Quick Pop Maker accessories, visit our online store at **zokuhome.com**.*

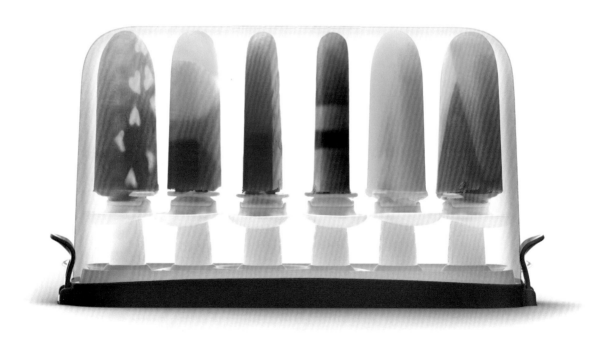

ENOUGH TALK...
LET'S MAKE
QUICK
POPS!™

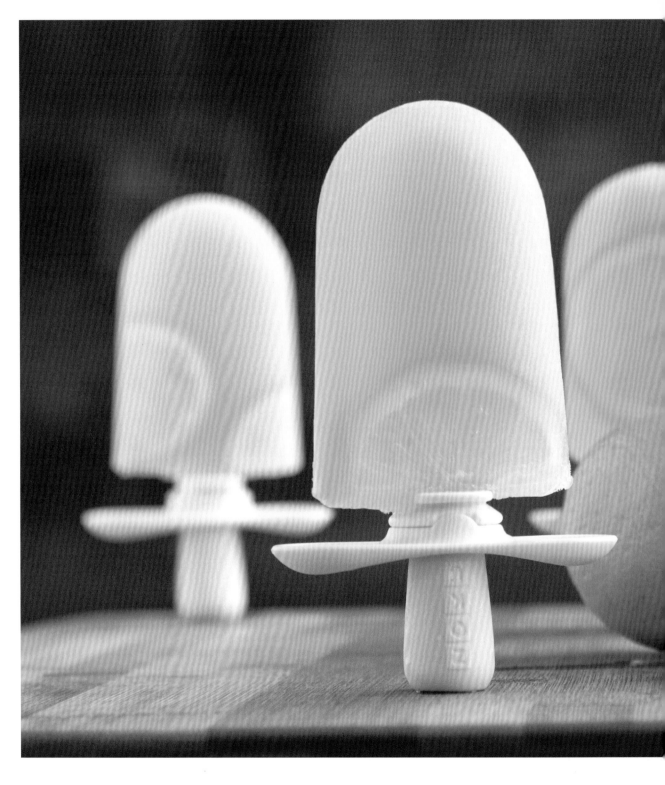

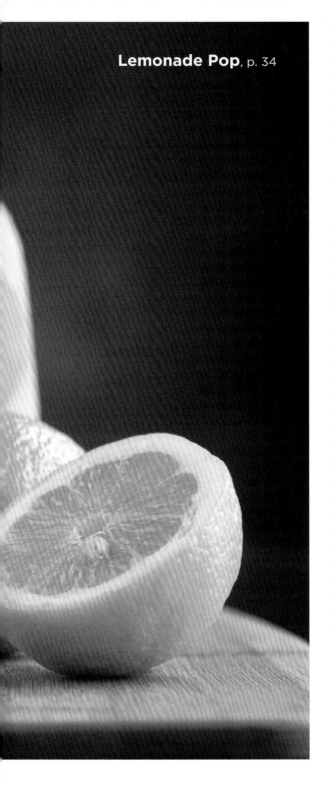

Lemonade Pop, p. 34

Fresh
& Fruity
Quick
Pops™

Lemonade

Pucker up!

INGREDIENTS

- 1 cup (8 oz) water
- 3 Tbsp sugar
- 1/4 cup (2 oz) fresh lemon juice
- 1/4 cup (2 oz) pure orange juice
- 1/4 tsp vanilla extract
- Lemon slices, cut 1/8" thick (optional)

MAKE THE LEMON BASE Stir together the water and sugar until sugar has dissolved (1–2 min.). Stir in the lemon juice, orange juice, and vanilla.

ASSEMBLE THE POPS Using the Zoku Fruit Wand (p. 12) or tweezers, apply the lemon slices to the walls of the pop maker molds. Insert sticks and pour the lemon base until you reach the fill line. Let freeze completely, then remove the pops with the Super Tool and enjoy! Repeat with remaining pops. Yields 6.

Watermelon

No summer BBQ would be complete without the sweet taste of watermelon. You won't want to spit out these watermelon "seeds" because they're delicious chocolate chips.

WATERMELON LAYER
- 8 oz seeded watermelon, chopped (about 15 1-inch cubes)
- 2 Tbsp plain lowfat yogurt
- 1 1/2 Tbsp agave nectar
- 1 1/2 Tbsp fresh lemon juice

LEMON LAYER
- 3 Tbsp whole milk
- 3 Tbsp water
- 1 1/2 Tbsp fresh lemon juice
- 1 1/2 Tbsp agave nectar
- 2 drops yellow food coloring and 1 drop green food coloring (optional)

EXTRAS
- 18 semi-sweet chocolate chips (optional)

MAKE WATERMELON LAYER Add watermelon to a blender and puree until smooth (about 30 seconds). Using a fine mesh sieve, strain the mixture into a bowl (using a spoon to scrape the sieve so it goes through faster). You should have about 1 cup + 2 Tbsp (9 oz) of the strained mixture. Whisk in the yogurt, agave, and lemon juice.

MAKE THE LEMON LAYER In a small bowl, stir together the milk, water, lemon juice, and agave. Transfer 2 Tbsp of the mixture to another small bowl and set aside. Add the food coloring to the remaining mixture and stir.

ASSEMBLE THE POPS Using tweezers, dip the chocolate chips into the watermelon layer and apply them to the walls of the pop maker molds, at least 1" below the fill line. Use 2-3 chips per pop. Insert sticks and pour the watermelon layer until you reach about 3/4" - 1" below the fill line. Let freeze completely, then pour 1 tsp of the uncolored lemon layer. Let freeze completely, then pour the green lemon layer until you reach the fill line. Let freeze completely, then remove the pops with the Super Tool and enjoy! Repeat with remaining pops. Yields 6.

Summertime
and the
livin's easy–

with these
peachy pops

Just Peachy

Enjoy all the tangy sweetness of peaches without dribbling juice down your chin.

INGREDIENTS
- 1 1/4 cup (7 oz) peeled, diced peaches (from 1–2 peaches)
- 1/2 cup (4 oz) peach nectar (store-bought)
- 3 Tbsp plain fat–free yogurt
- 1 1/2 tsp agave nectar
- 1 1/2 tsp fresh lime juice

MAKE THE PEACH BASE Combine the ingredients in a blender and puree until smooth.

ASSEMBLE THE POPS Insert sticks into the pop maker molds and pour peach base until you reach the fill line. Let freeze completely, then remove pops with the Super Tool and enjoy! Repeat with remaining pops. Yields 6.

Summer Morning

Biting into this pop will give you the sensation of taking a morning stroll out to your garden to pick some basil, the feeling of cool dew swept from blades of grass onto your bare feet. See photo, p 22.

INGREDIENTS
- 9 oz honeydew melon, chopped (about 18 1-inch cubes)
- 1/4 cup (2 oz) fresh lime juice
- 4 large fresh basil leaves
- 3 Tbsp water
- 1 Tbsp + 2 tsp sugar
- Sanding sugar (optional)

MAKE THE POP BASE Combine the ingredients except for sanding sugar in a blender and puree for 30–60 seconds or until basil leaves are fully broken down.

ASSEMBLE THE POPS Insert sticks into the pop maker molds and pour the pop base until you reach the fill line. Let freeze completely, then remove pops with the Super Tool. Sprinkle pops with sanding sugar immediately before serving & enjoy! Repeat with remaining pops. Yields 6.

Strawberry
Banana

STRAWBERRY LAYER

- 1 $\frac{1}{8}$ cup (6 oz) hulled, quartered strawberries
- 1 Tbsp fresh lemon juice
- 2 Tbsp lowfat vanilla yogurt
- 1 Tbsp 2% milk
- 2 Tbsp sugar

FIRST, MAKE THE STRAWBERRY LAYER

Combine strawberries and lemon juice in a blender and puree until smooth. Using a fine mesh sieve, strain the mixture into a medium bowl (using a spoon to scrape the sieve so it goes through faster). You should have about $\frac{2}{3}$ cup (5 $\frac{1}{2}$ oz) of the strained mixture. Whisk in yogurt, milk, and sugar until sugar has dissolved.

FREEZE THE STRAWBERRY LAYER

Insert sticks into the pop maker molds and pour strawberry layer halfway up the mold (using about 2 Tbsp per pop). Immediately tilt the pop maker on a slight angle and hold it tilted for 1 minute. Then set it down flat and let freeze completely.

BANANA LAYER

- $\frac{3}{4}$ cup (6 oz) mashed ripe banana, (peel should have some black spots)
- 2 Tbsp 2% milk
- 1 $\frac{1}{2}$ Tbsp fresh lemon juice
- 1 Tbsp sugar

THEN MAKE THE BANANA LAYER

Combine the banana layer ingredients in a blender and puree until smooth and sugar has dissolved.

AND FREEZE THE BANANA LAYER

Pour banana layer into the prepared pop maker molds until you reach the fill line. Let freeze completely, then remove the pops with the Super Tool and enjoy! Repeat with remaining pops. Yields 6.

Pop Tip

If you let the banana layer sit for too long, it will start to turn brown, so it is best used right away.

Why choose **one flavor** when you can have **two** at the same time!

This coconut pop's
gone bananas!

Caramelized
Banana
Coconut

INGREDIENTS
- 1 Tbsp butter
- 1 Tbsp brown sugar
- 1 ripe banana, peeled (5 oz)
- 3/4 cup + 2 Tbsp (7 oz) 2% milk
- 1/4 cup (2 oz) plain fat–free yogurt
- 1 Tbsp honey
- 3/4 tsp coconut extract
- Pinch cinnamon (just under 1/8 tsp)
- 3 Tbsp coconut flakes, toasted
  (toasting instructions, p. 79)

MAKE THE POP BASE Melt butter and brown sugar in a non–stick skillet over low heat; stir until it starts to thicken. Cut banana into 1-inch pieces, add to skillet, and stir to coat. Remove from heat and mash to incorporate excess butter and sugar. It should measure 1/2 cup. Whisk in the milk, yogurt, honey, coconut extract, and cinnamon. Refrigerate until cool.

ASSEMBLE THE POPS Insert sticks into the pop maker molds and pour the pop base, pausing to add pinches of coconut on each side of the sticks as you pour. Let freeze completely, then remove the pops with the Super Tool and enjoy! Repeat with remaining pops. Yields 6.

Mango

Start out with a ripe mango– you can tell it's ripe if it is slightly soft to the touch and has a sweet aroma. Like peaches, mangoes can be coaxed into ripening by placing them inside a paper bag. Take care when removing the flat seed from this mischievously slippery fruit.

INGREDIENTS
- 1 mango (about 14 oz whole), peeled & seed removed
- 1 navel orange (about 12 oz whole), peeled, seeded
- 1 red delicious apple (about 8 oz whole), peeled & cored
- 1/3 ripe banana, peeled (about 2 oz)
- Sliver of lemon, rind & seeds removed

MAKE THE POP BASE Juice all fruit in a juicer according to the manufacturer's instructions; stir to combine juices.

ASSEMBLE POPS Insert sticks into the pop maker molds and pour the mango base until you reach the fill line. Let freeze completely, then remove the pops with the Super Tool and enjoy! Repeat with remaining pops. Yields 6.

Bananaberry

Bananas and berries join forces in this healthy, refreshing pop that's naturally packed with good-for-you antioxidants.

INGREDIENTS
- $3/4$ cup (3 $1/2$ oz) blueberries
- $1/2$ cup (2 $1/2$ oz) blackberries
- 1 peeled banana (4 oz), divided
- 1 cup (8 oz) pure apple juice (store-bought)
- 2 tsp agave nectar

MAKE THE POP BASE Combine the berries and $1/2$ of the banana in a blender and puree until smooth. Using a fine mesh sieve, strain the mixture into a medium bowl (using a spoon to scrape the sieve so it goes through faster). You should have about $2/3$ cup (5 $1/2$ oz) of the strained mixture. Stir in the apple juice and agave.

ASSEMBLE THE POPS Slice the remaining $1/2$ banana into $1/8$" thick slices. Using the Zoku Fruit Wand (p. 12) or tweezers, apply the banana slices to the walls of the pop maker molds. Insert sticks and pour the pop base until you reach the fill line. Let freeze completely, then remove the pops with the Super Tool and enjoy! Repeat with remaining pops. Yields 6.

Black Raspberry Zig zag

Run zig zags, hop the couch– do whatever it takes to get to your Quick Pop Maker fast enough for one of these gorgeous and super-tasty berry pops. Sour cream may at first seem an unlikely ingredient, but it lends a refreshing creaminess that balances out the tart berries. See photo and layering technique, p. 21.

RASPBERRY LAYER
- 1 cup (5 oz) raspberries
- 1/4 cup (2 oz) 2% milk
- 1 tsp vanilla extract
- 1 Tbsp sour cream
- 2 Tbsp sugar

BLACKBERRY LAYER
- 1 cup (5 oz) blackberries
- 1/4 cup + 2 Tbsp (3 oz) 2% milk
- 1 tsp vanilla extract
- 1 Tbsp sour cream
- 1 Tbsp + 1 tsp sugar

MAKE THE RASPBERRY LAYER Combine the raspberries, milk, and vanilla in a blender and puree until smooth. Using a fine mesh sieve, strain the mixture into a medium bowl (using a spoon to scrape the sieve so it goes faster). You should have about 3/4 cup (6 oz) of the strained mixture. Whisk in the sour cream and sugar until sugar has dissolved.

MAKE THE BLACKBERRY LAYER Combine the blackberries, milk, and vanilla in a blender and puree until smooth. Using a fine mesh sieve, strain the mixture into a medium bowl (using a spoon to scrape the sieve so it goes faster). You should have about 3/4 cup (6 oz) of the strained mixture. Whisk in the sour cream and sugar until sugar has dissolved.

ASSEMBLE THE POPS Use the Zoku Angle Tray (p. 12) to set the pop maker at an angle. Insert sticks into the pop maker molds and pour the raspberry layer about 1/4 way up the molds (using about 1 Tbsp per pop). Let freeze completely, then flip the pop maker around so it's angled in the opposite direction and pour the blackberry layer to reach about halfway up the mold (using about 1 Tbsp per pop). Let freeze completely and repeat layering once more or until you reach the fill line. Let freeze completely, then remove the pops with the Super Tool and enjoy! Repeat with remaining pops. Yields 6.

Rhuberry

Rhubarb + Strawberry = Rhuberry!

RHUBARB
- $1/4$ cup sugar
- 3 Tbsp water
- 4 oz rhubarb

POP BASE
- $1/3$ cup (1 $1/2$ oz) hulled, quartered strawberries
- $1/2$ cup (4 oz) water
- $1/4$ cup (2 oz) pure orange juice
- 2 tsp agave nectar
- Thin strips of peeled strawberry skin (optional)

PREPARE THE RHUBARB Remove and discard any leaves from rhubarb and cut stalks into $1/2$" pieces. In a small, non-aluminum saucepan over medium-low heat, combine the sugar and water; bring to a boil, stirring frequently. Add the rhubarb and lower the heat to a simmer. Simmer until rhubarb is tender (about 3-5 min). Refrigerate until cool.

MAKE THE POP BASE Transfer the cooled rhubarb mixture to a blender, add strawberries, and puree until smooth. Pour mixture into a medium bowl and whisk in the water, orange juice, and agave.

ASSEMBLE THE POPS Using the Zoku Fruit Wand (p. 12) or tweezers, apply the strawberry skins to the walls of the pop maker molds. If they are not sticking, dip them into the pop base, pat dry with a paper towel and re-apply. Insert sticks into the prepared pop maker molds, and pour the pop base until you reach the fill line. Let freeze completely, then remove pops with the Super Tool and enjoy! Repeat with remaining pops. Yields 6.

Pink Mojito

Ice pops may bring out the kid in you, but you'll feel sophisticated while savoring this cocktail-inspired pop. Surprisingly, even grapefruit skeptics are won over by this recipe.

INGREDIENTS

- 2/3 cup (5 1/2 oz) water
- 3 Tbsp sugar
- 7 fresh mint leaves
- 1 cup + 2 Tbsp (9 oz) pure pink grapefruit juice (store-bought or about 2 grape-fruits, juiced)

Pop Tip

When juicing grapefruit, remove as much of the rind and the inner white pith as possible to prevent bitter tasting juice.

MAKE THE MINT SYRUP In a small sauce-pan over medium-low heat, combine the water, sugar, and fresh mint leaves. Bring to a simmer, cover, reduce heat to low, and continue to simmer for about 5 minutes. Remove from heat. Using a fine mesh sieve, strain the mixture into a medium bowl. Refrigerate until cool.

MAKE THE POP BASE Stir together the cooled mint syrup and grapefruit juice.

ASSEMBLE THE POPS Insert sticks into the pop maker molds and pour the pop base until you reach the fill line. Let freeze com-pletely, then remove pops with the Super Tool and enjoy! Repeat with remaining pops. Yields 6.

Pining for Papaya

Sit back and daydream about a lazy day at the beach while cooling off with this ice-cold tropical treat. See photo, p. 20.

PINEAPPLE LAYER

- 3/4 cup (6 oz) pure pineapple juice (store-bought)
- 2 tsp agave nectar
- 1 1/2 tsp fresh lime juice
- 1/4 tsp coconut extract

PAPAYA LAYER

- 4 oz seeded, chopped papaya (about half of a small Hawaiian papaya)
- 1/4 cup + 2 Tbsp (3 oz) pure pineapple juice (store-bought)
- 1 tsp fresh lime juice
- 1 tsp agave nectar

MAKE THE PINEAPPLE LAYER Stir together the pineapple layer ingredients.

MAKE THE PAPAYA LAYER Combine all papaya layer ingredients in a blender and puree until smooth.

ASSEMBLE THE POPS Insert sticks into the pop maker molds and pour the pineapple mixture halfway up the molds (using about 2 Tbsp per pop). Let freeze completely, then pour the papaya layer until you reach the fill line. Let freeze completely, then remove pops with the Super Tool and enjoy! Repeat with remaining pops. Yields 6.

Kiwi Cherry

Red and green may normally conjure thoughts of Christmas, but even in the cold winter this fruity pop will make it feel like summer– at least, until it's been devoured!

KIWI LAYER
- 1 ½ ripe kiwis
- ½ cup (4 oz) pure apple juice (store-bought)
- 2 tsp agave nectar

CHERRY LAYER
- ¼ cup + 2 Tbsp (3 oz) pure apple juice (store-bought)
- ¼ cup + 2 Tbsp (3 oz) pure black cherry juice (store-bought)
- 1 tsp agave nectar

MAKE THE KIWI LAYER Combine the kiwi layer ingredients in a blender and puree until smooth.

MAKE THE CHERRY LAYER Stir together the cherry layer ingredients.

ASSEMBLE THE POPS Insert sticks into the pop maker molds and pour the kiwi layer half-way up the molds (using about 2 Tbsp per pop). Let freeze completely, then pour the cherry layer until you reach the fill line. Let freeze completely, then remove pops with the Super Tool and enjoy! Repeat with remaining pops. Yields 6.

Cookie Dough (left)
& Cookies & Cream (right), p. 52

I Scream
for
**Quick
Pops!**™

Cookies & Cream

Ah, to dunk or not to dunk? There is no debate here where whole cookies are deeply immersed in a vanilla base that's full of chocolate wafer crumbs.

INGREDIENTS

- 3 chocolate sandwich cookies, twisted apart into halves
- 1 recipe vanilla base, p. 57
- $^1/_4$ cup crumbled chocolate wafers

ASSEMBLE THE POPS Dip the decorative side of half a sandwich cookie in the vanilla base and pat dry with a paper towel. Using the Zoku Fruit Wand (p. 12) or tweezers, apply the dipped cookie to the wall of the pop maker mold. Insert the stick and repeat with remaining molds.

Divide the vanilla base and cookie crumbs in half; add one portion of the crumbled wafers to one portion of the vanilla base. Immediately pour the vanilla–cookie mixture into the prepared molds until you reach the fill line. Let freeze completely, then remove pops with the Super Tool and enjoy! Repeat with remaining pops. Yields 6.

Cookie Dough

Sneaking a bite of cookie dough from the mixing bowl feels a little wrong. But adding it to a pop with a creamy vanilla base? So wrong, it's right!

INGREDIENTS

- Cookie dough*, approx. enough for 2 cookies, cut into 36 pieces ($^1/_4$" squares, $^1/_8$" thick)
- 1 recipe vanilla base, p. 57

ASSEMBLE THE POPS Using the Zoku Fruit Wand (p. 12), apply the cookie dough pieces to the walls of the pop maker molds (using 6 pieces per pop). Insert sticks and pour the vanilla base until you reach the fill line. Let freeze completely, then remove pops with the Super Tool and enjoy! Repeat with remaining pops. Yields 6.

* Consumption of raw eggs poses a risk of *Salmonella* food poisoning which is higher for people who are pregnant, elderly, very young or who have impaired immune systems. To protect against this risk, use your own eggless cookie dough or commercially available cookie dough that is made with pasteurized eggs.

Neapolitan

The colors of this pop look great together whether you pour them as flat layers or make fun angles using our angle tray. Feel free to mix it up, just beware of the Neapolitan die-hards who swear that the vanilla simply must go in the middle. See photo, p. 9.

STRAWBERRY LAYER
- $1/2$ cup + $1/8$ cup (3 $1/2$ oz) hulled, quartered strawberries
- 3 Tbsp whole milk
- 1 Tbsp sour cream
- 1 Tbsp + 1 tsp sugar
- 1 $1/2$ tsp vanilla extract
- $1/2$ tsp heavy cream

VANILLA LAYER
- $1/4$ cup + 2 Tbsp (3 oz) 2% milk
- 2 $1/2$ Tbsp heavy cream
- 1 $1/2$ Tbsp sugar
- 1 $1/2$ tsp vanilla extract

CHOCOLATE LAYER
- $1/3$ cup (2 $1/2$ oz) whole milk
- 2 $1/2$ Tbsp chocolate syrup
- 1 Tbsp heavy cream
- 1 $1/2$ tsp water
- $1/4$ tsp vanilla extract

MAKE THE STRAWBERRY LAYER
Combine the strawberries and milk in a blender and puree until smooth. Using a fine mesh sieve, strain the mixture into a small bowl (using a spoon to scrape the sieve so it goes through faster). You should have about $1/4$ cup + 3 Tbsp (3 $1/2$ oz) of the strained mixture. Whisk in the sour cream, sugar, vanilla, and heavy cream until sugar has dissolved. Insert sticks into the pop maker molds and pour the strawberry layer $1/3$ of the way up the molds (using about 1 Tbsp + 1 tsp per pop). Let freeze completely.

MAKE THE VANILLA LAYER Whisk together the vanilla layer ingredients until sugar has dissolved. Pour the vanilla layer into the prepared molds until it reaches $2/3$ of the way up the mold (using about 1 Tbsp + 1 tsp per pop). Let freeze completely.

MAKE THE CHOCOLATE LAYER Whisk together the chocolate layer ingredients. Pour the chocolate layer into the prepared molds until you reach the fill line. Let freeze completely, then remove pops with the Super Tool and enjoy! Repeat with remaining pops. Yields 6.

Chai

Energize yourself with this spicy little number!

INGREDIENTS

- 1 1/2 cups + 2 Tbsp (13 oz) whole milk, divided
- 1 star anise star
- 5 whole cloves
- 1 cinnamon stick
- 5 whole white peppercorns
- 1 cardamom pod
- 1 pinch salt
- 2 tsp full-bodied black tea, whole leaf
- 1/4 cup (2 oz) half & half
- 2 Tbsp + 1 tsp honey

MAKE THE CHAI BASE With the flat side of a knife, press firmly on the cardamom pod to open it slightly, revealing the seeds. In a small, heavy saucepan over medium heat, combine 1 cup (8 oz) of the milk, the chai spices (anise star through cardamom), and the salt. Heat the mixture, whisking occasionally, just until steamy (do not boil). Reduce heat to low, cover, and continue to simmer for 25 minutes.

Remove the mixture from heat and add the tea; cover and let steep for 6 minutes. Using a fine mesh sieve, strain the mixture into a bowl; discard the tea and spices. You should have about 2/3 cup (5 1/2 oz) of the strained mixture. Stir in the honey until fully dissolved. Then stir in the half & half and the remaining 1/2 cup + 2 Tbsp (5 oz) of the whole milk. Refrigerate until cool.

ASSEMBLE THE POPS Insert sticks into the pop maker molds and pour the cooled chai base until you reach the fill line. Let freeze completely, then remove pops with the Super Tool and enjoy! Repeat with remaining pops. Yields 6.

Tartufo

Tartufo is an ice cream dessert that's ever-present on Italian-American restaurant menus. It's traditionally a scoop of vanilla ice cream that has maraschino cherries hiding on the inside and a hard chocolate shell on the outside. We brought this tasty combo to new life as a pop.

VANILLA BASE

- 8 oz vanilla pudding
  (2 individual serving cups)
- ½ cup (4 oz) water
- 3 Tbsp sugar
- 1 Tbsp vanilla extract

EXTRAS

- 12 maraschino cherries, cut into quarters
- 6 maraschino cherries, bottoms cut in half but still intact (see cherry on top of the pop in the photo)
- 1 recipe Chocolate Quick Shell, p. 29

MAKE THE VANILLA BASE Whisk together the vanilla base ingredients until sugar has dissolved.

ASSEMBLE THE POPS Using the Zoku Fruit Wand (p. 12) or tweezers, apply the quartered cherries to the sides of the pop maker molds (using 8 quarters per pop)*. Insert sticks and pour the vanilla base until you reach the fill line. Let freeze completely, then remove the pops with the Super Tool. Repeat with remaining pops.

DECORATE THE POPS Dip the pops half-way into the Chocolate Quick Shell and immediately garnish with a halved cherry on top. Wait a few seconds for the shell to harden completely and enjoy! Repeat with remaining pops. Yields 6.

* For an easier method, you can just add the cherries in as you pour the base. This way is faster, but the cherry pieces may not show through as much on the outside of the pops.

Coffee Buzz

Some people take their coffee black, while others prefer four sugars. This recipe is sweetened to a happy medium, but taste it before freezing and sweeten it to your preference.

INGREDIENTS

- 1 1/3 cup (10 1/2 oz) 2% milk
- 1/4 cup sugar
- 2 Tbsp instant espresso powder
- 1/3 cup (2 1/2 oz) heavy cream

MAKE THE COFFEE BASE In a medium saucepan over low heat, warm the milk (do not boil). Whisk in the espresso powder and sugar until dissolved. Remove from heat and let cool slightly (about 10 min). Stir in the heavy cream. Refrigerate until cool, stirring occasionally to prevent a skin from forming.

ASSEMBLE THE POPS Insert sticks into the pop maker molds and pour the cooled coffee base until you reach the fill line. Let freeze completely, then remove pops with the Super Tool and enjoy! Repeat with remaining pops. Yields 6.

Butter Pecan

INGREDIENTS

- 3/4 cup pecan halves
- 1/2 Tbsp salted butter
- 1 Tbsp brown sugar
- 3/4 cup (6 oz) water
- 2 1/2 oz butterscotch chips (just under 1/2 cup)
- 1/2 cup (4 oz) half & half
- 1/2 tsp vanilla extract

TOAST THE PECANS In a small non-stick pan over medium-low heat, combine pecans, butter and brown sugar; stir for about 3 minutes until the nuts are just toasted (do not burn). Let cool completely.

MAKE THE POP BASE In a small saucepan over low heat, whisk together the water and butterscotch chips until the chips have just melted (do not boil). Remove from heat and let cool slightly (about 10 min.). Stir in the half & half and vanilla. Refrigerate until cool, whisking occasionally to prevent a skin from forming.

ASSEMBLE THE POPS Insert sticks into the pop maker molds and add the cooled pecans on each side of the sticks until you reach the fill line (using 6–8 pecan halves per pop). Pour the cooled pop base until you reach the fill line. Let freeze completely, then remove pops with the Super Tool and enjoy! Repeat with remaining pops. Yields 6.

Mix up your morning routine
with this pick-me-up pop!

Mint Chip

Mint and chocolate are a match made in dessert heaven. This creamy, minty pop was born to be dipped in our Chocolate Quick Shell.

MINT BASE

- 1 ½ cups (12 oz) whole milk
- 3 Tbsp agave nectar
- 1 tsp peppermint extract
- ½ tsp vanilla extract
- Pinch salt

EXTRAS

- ¼ cup semi-sweet chocolate chips
- 1 recipe Chocolate Quick Shell, p. 29

MAKE THE MINT BASE Whisk together the mint base ingredients.

ASSEMBLE POPS Using tweezers, dip the chocolate chips into the mint base and apply them to the walls of the pop maker molds. Insert sticks and pour the mint base into the prepared molds until you reach the fill line. Let freeze completely, then remove pops with the Super Tool. Repeat with remaining pops.

APPLY THE QUICK SHELL Dip pops into the Chocolate Quick Shell; wait a few seconds for the shell to harden completely and enjoy! Yields 6.

Pistachio

Friends will be green with envy if you devour this flavorful pistachio pop in front of them. So try to share - we know, it's hard.

INGREDIENTS

- 1 cup (8 oz) water
- 1/4 cup (2 oz) half & half
- 1/4 cup vanilla pudding
- 1/4 cup + 1 Tbsp sugar
- 1/3 cup ground pistachios* (raw, shelled)
- 2 tsp almond extract

* Add pistachios to a food processor and process until fine.

MAKE THE PISTACHIO BASE Combine all ingredients in a blender and puree until pistachios are incorporated (1–2 min.). Using a cheese cloth that's doubled over, strain the mixture into a medium bowl. You should have about 1 1/2 cups (12 oz) of the strained mixture.

ASSEMBLE THE POPS Insert sticks into the pop maker molds and pour the pistachio base until you reach the fill line. Let freeze completely, then remove pops with the Super Tool and enjoy! Repeat with remaining pops. Yields 6.

Pop Tip

Cheese cloth is a necessary tool for making this pop; it strains out the small pieces of pistachio and absorbs some of the nut oils, helping the pop freeze fast!

Don't be fooled by the cool, calm color of these Pistachio pops...

...they are **packed** with flavor.

Chocolate-Coated Cinnamon Crunch

Crunchy cinnamon cereal is pretty delicious in it's own right, so imagine how great it tastes after you coat it in dark chocolate and add it to a creamy vanilla ice pop. You may have some of the chocolate–coated cereal mixture leftover after you make the pops, but trust us– you'll be happy for the leftovers!

INGREDIENTS

- 1 $\frac{1}{2}$ oz bittersweet chocolate
- $\frac{3}{4}$ cups cinnamon crunch cereal
- 1 Tbsp sugar
- 1 $\frac{1}{4}$ tsp cinnamon, divided
- 1 recipe vanilla base, p. 57

MAKE THE CHOCOLATE CRUNCH Line a baking sheet with waxed or parchment paper and set aside. In a medium, micro-wave–safe bowl, microwave the chocolate on high for 20 seconds. Stir and microwave in 10–second increments until just melted. Add the cereal and stir gently until it is completely coated. Spread the mixture out in a single layer on the prepared baking sheet. Transfer it to the refrigerator to cool until the chocolate is set and just firm to the touch (about 20 min).

Remove cereal mixture from the refrigerator and go over it with a knife, chopping it into pieces ($\frac{1}{4}$" x $\frac{1}{4}$" or less). In a large ziptop bag, combine the sugar and 1 tsp of the cinnamon; shake to combine. Add the cooled, chopped cereal mixture to the bag and shake until it is coated with the cinnamon sugar. Set aside.

MAKE THE POP BASE Whisk together the vanilla base and the remaining $\frac{1}{4}$ tsp of the cinnamon.

ASSEMBLE THE POPS Insert sticks into the pop maker molds and pour a drop of the pop base into each mold (using about $\frac{1}{2}$ Tbsp per pop). Add some of the cereal mixture on each side of the sticks, pushing down with a chopstick if necessary. Pour a little of the pop base. Repeat, fitting in as much of the cereal mixture as you can, until you reach the fill line. Let freeze completely, then remove the pops with the Super Tool and enjoy! Repeat with remaining pops. Yields 6.

From left to right: **Apple Pie à la Mode**, p. 69;
Key Lime Pie p. 76; **Pumpkin Pie,** p. 68

Bake Shop Quick Pops™

Pumpkin Pie

The Pilgrims discovered many new things, so how would they feel upon encountering this Pumpkin Pie Pop? We suspect they'd approve! Photo, p. 67.

PUMPKIN LAYER

- $1/4$ cup + 1 Tbsp (2 $1/2$ oz) canned pumpkin pie mix
- $3/4$ cup (6 oz) whole milk
- 2 Tbsp half & half
- 1 $1/2$ tsp brown sugar
- $1/4$ tsp vanilla extract

VANILLA LAYER

- $1/4$ cup vanilla pudding
- $1/4$ cup (2 oz) whole milk
- 1 tsp sugar
- $1/8$ tsp vanilla extract

EXTRAS

- $1/4$ cup crumbled ginger snaps

MAKE THE PUMPKIN LAYER Whisk together the pumpkin layer ingredients until sugar has dissolved.

MAKE THE VANILLA LAYER Whisk together the vanilla layer ingredients until sugar has dissolved.

ASSEMBLE THE POPS Insert sticks into the pop maker molds and pour the pumpkin layer $1/4$ way up the molds (using about 1 Tbsp per pop). Let freeze completely, then add the crumbled ginger snaps (using about 1 tsp per pop), packing down with the blunt end of a chopstick to create a dense layer. Pour some of the vanilla layer (using about 2 tsp per pop) and let freeze completely. Alternate layering as desired until you reach the fill line, ending with the pumpkin or vanilla layer (not ginger snaps). Let freeze completely, then remove pops with the Super Tool and enjoy! Repeat with remaining pops. Yields 6.

Apple Pie à la Mode

You may think that apple pie has to be served warm, but prepare to be converted with one bite of this all-American pop. Photo, p. 66.

APPLE LAYER
- $1/2$ cup (4 oz) plain unsweetened apple sauce
- $1/2$ cup (4 oz) apple cider
- 1 Tbsp brown sugar
- 1 pinch cinnamon

VANILLA LAYER
- $1/2$ cup (4 oz) half & half
- 2 tsp agave nectar
- $1/4$ tsp vanilla extract

EXTRAS
- $1/4$ cup crumbled graham crackers

MAKE THE APPLE LAYER Whisk together the apple layer ingredients until sugar has dissolved.

MAKE THE VANILLA LAYER Stir together the vanilla layer ingredients.

ASSEMBLE POPS Insert sticks into the pop maker molds and pour a drop of the vanilla layer (using about 2 tsp per pop). Let freeze completely, then add the crumbled graham crackers (using about 1 tsp per pop), packing down with the blunt end of a chopstick to create a dense layer. Pour some of the apple layer (using about 1 $1/2$ Tbsp per pop) and let freeze completely. Alternate layering as desired until you reach the fill line, ending with the apple or vanilla layer (not graham crackers). Let freeze completely, then remove pops with the Super Tool and enjoy! Repeat with remaining pops. Yields 6.

This pop
takes the cake!

Strawberry Shortpop

For a dairy–free version, try replacing the 2% milk with rice milk and substituting vegan pudding for regular pudding.

STRAWBERRY SAUCE
- $3/4$ cup (4 oz) hulled, quartered strawberries
- $3/4$ tsp water
- 2 tsp honey
- $1/8$ tsp vanilla extract

VANILLA BASE
- 8 oz vanilla pudding (2 individual serving cups)
- $1/2$ cup (4 oz) whole or 2% milk
- 1 $1/2$ Tbsp sugar
- $3/4$ tsp vanilla extract

EXTRAS
- 2 strawberries, hulled & sliced lengthwise into $1/8$" thick slices
- 1 ($1/4$" thick) slice plain pound cake, cut into 36 ($1/4$" x $1/4$" x $1/4$") pieces

MAKE THE STRAWBERRY SAUCE Combine the strawberries and water in a blender and puree until smooth. Using a fine mesh sieve, strain the mixture into a small bowl (using a spoon to scrape it so it goes through faster). You should have almost $1/2$ cup (4 oz) of the strained mixture. Whisk in the honey and vanilla.

MAKE THE VANILLA BASE Whisk together the vanilla base ingredients until sugar has dissolved.

ASSEMBLE THE POPS Using the Zoku Fruit Wand (p. 12) or tweezers, apply the strawberry slices to the walls of the pop maker molds. Insert sticks into the pop maker molds and add a piece of pound cake on each side of the sticks. Pour the vanilla layer about $1/3$ way up the prepared molds (using about 1 $1/2$ Tbsp per pop). Immediately add a layer of strawberry sauce (using about 1 tsp per pop). Repeat twice more or until you reach the fill line. Let freeze completely, then remove pops with the Super Tool and enjoy! Repeat with remaining pops. Yields 6.

Coconut Macaroon

Macaroons are the ultimate treat for any coconut lover. Say hello to that sweet coconut cookie, in pop form.

COCONUT BASE
- 3/4 cup + 2 Tbsp (7 oz) coconut milk (not lite)
- 1/4 cup (2 oz) 2% milk
- 3 Tbsp water
- 3 Tbsp + 1 tsp sugar

EXTRAS
- 1/2 cup shredded sweetened coconut

MAKE THE COCONUT BASE Whisk together the coconut base ingredients until sugar has dissolved.

ASSEMBLE THE POPS Insert sticks into the pop maker molds and pour the coconut base, pausing to add large pinches of coconut on each side of the sticks as you pour (using about 1 1/2 Tbsp coconut per pop). Repeat until you reach the fill line, topping the filled mold with a pinch of coconut to create a skirt (see p. 13). Let freeze completely, then remove the pops with the Super Tool and enjoy! Repeat with remaining pops. Yields 6.

Choconut

If you prefer a more indulgent macaroon, our coconut pop tastes great with a coating of our Chocolate Quick Shell and a little added crunch from toasted almonds.

INGREDIENTS
- 1/4 cup sliced almonds
- 1 recipe Coconut Macaroon (left)
- 1 recipe Chocolate Quick Shell, p. 29.

TOAST THE NUTS In a non-stick pan over medium-low heat, add the nuts and heat for 3–5 minutes until fragrant and golden brown (do not burn). Immediately remove from pan and let cool completely.

ASSEMBLE THE POPS Follow instructions for Coconut Macaroon assembly (left), dropping large pinches of coconut and a few almond slices on each side of the sticks as you pour the pop base.

APPLY THE QUICK SHELL Dip pops in the Chocolate Quick Shell; wait a few seconds for the shell to harden completely and enjoy! Repeat with remaining pops. Yields 6.

Carrot Cake

This carrot cake pop is the real deal: carrots, spices, pineapple, coconut and most importantly, cream cheese icing!

CREAM CHEESE LAYER

- 1 1/2 Tbsp cream cheese, room temp
- 1/4 cup + 2 Tbsp (3 oz) whole milk, lukewarm
- 1 1/2 Tbsp confectioners' sugar
- 1/4 tsp vanilla extract

CARROT LAYER

- 1/2 cup (4 oz) pure carrot juice (or about 4 medium carrots, juiced)
- 1/4 cup + 2 Tbsp (3 oz) pure apple juice
- 1/4 cup minced fresh pineapple
- 1 Tbsp agave nectar
- 1/2 tsp ginger juice (store-bought or juiced ginger root)
- Pinch cinnamon, to taste

EXTRAS

- 1 tsp finely shredded coconut flakes, toasted (toasting instructions, p. 79)
- 1/4 cup crumbled graham crackers

MAKE THE CREAM CHEESE LAYER In a small, microwave-safe bowl, whisk the cream cheese until smooth. Add the milk and whisk slowly (to prevent bubbles from forming) until the cream cheese is completely incorporated. If clumps of cream cheese remain intact, microwave the mixture in 10–second increments, whisking in between until they dissipate. Whisk in the sugar and vanilla until sugar has dissolved. Refrigerate until completely cooled.

MAKE THE CARROT LAYER Stir together the carrot layer ingredients.

ASSEMBLE THE POPS Insert sticks into the pop maker molds and pour a drop of the cream cheese layer (using about 1/2 Tbsp per pop). Let freeze completely, then add the crumbled graham crackers (using 1 tsp per pop) and a pinch of toasted coconut on each side of sticks; pack down with the blunt end of a chopstick to create a dense layer. Pour carrot layer until you reach halfway up the molds (using about 1 1/2 Tbsp per pop), making sure to encourage an even flow of minced pineapple as you pour. Let freeze completely. Repeat layering as desired until you reach the fill line, ending with the carrot or cream cheese layer (not graham crackers). Let freeze completely, then remove pops with the Super Tool and enjoy! Repeat with remaining pops. Yields 6.

Key Lime Pie

This tasty pop is soon to become the official frozen treat of the Florida Keys (we hope, anyway). Key limes have a different flavor from the more common Persian lime. If you can't find fresh key limes, bottled juice will do just fine. See photo, p. 66.

KEY LIME BASE

- 1 cup (8 oz) whole milk
- 1/4 cup sweetened condensed milk
- 1/4 cup (2 oz) pure key lime juice, fresh or store–bought
- 2 Tbsp clover honey

EXTRAS

- lime slices, cut 1/8" thick (optional)
- 1/4 cup crumbled graham crackers

MAKE THE KEY LIME BASE Whisk together the key lime base ingredients.

ASSEMBLE THE POPS Using the Zoku Fruit Wand (p. 12) or tweezers, apply the lime slices to the walls of the pop maker molds. Insert sticks and pour key lime base 1/2 way up the molds (using about 2 Tbsp per pop). Let freeze completely, then add 1 tsp of the crumbled graham crackers to each mold, packing down with the blunt end of a chopstick to create a dense layer. Repeat layering as desired until you reach the fill line, ending with the key lime base (not graham crackers). Let freeze completely, then remove pops with the Super Tool and enjoy! Repeat with remaining pops. Yields 6.

Marble Cheesecake

Two flavors of rich cheesecake blended together. Does it get much better than that?

BASIC CHEESECAKE LAYER
- 1/4 cup cream cheese, room temp
- 1/2 cup (4 oz) 2% milk, lukewarm
- 2 Tbsp + 1 tsp sugar
- 2 tsp vanilla extract
- 1 1/4 tsp white wine vinegar

CHOCOLATE CHEESECAKE LAYER
- 1/2 cup (4 oz) 2% milk
- 3 Tbsp water
- 1 oz bittersweet chocolate, chopped
- 3 Tbsp sugar
- 2 Tbsp cream cheese, room temp, beaten
- 1 tsp white wine vinegar
- 3/4 tsp vanilla extract

MAKE THE BASIC CHEESECAKE LAYER In a medium, microwave–safe bowl, whisk the cream cheese until smooth. Add the milk and whisk slowly (to prevent bubbles from forming) until the milk is completely incorporated. If clumps of cream cheese remain intact, microwave the mixture in 15–second increments, whisking in between until they dissipate. Whisk in the sugar, vanilla, and vinegar until sugar has dissolved. Refrigerate until cool.

MAKE THE CHOCOLATE CHEESECAKE LAYER In a small saucepan over very low heat, whisk together the milk, water, chocolate, and sugar until the chocolate has completely melted (do not boil) and chocolate granules have dissolved, about 5 minutes (test by dipping a clean spoon into the mixture; if you don't see many chocolate specks, it's ready to come off the heat). Let cool to lukewarm (about 15 min.) and then whisk in the cream cheese. If clumps of cream cheese remain intact, put the mixture back on very low heat for about 1 min., whisking until clumps dissipate (do not heat for too long or it will thicken). Whisk in the vinegar and vanilla. Refrigerate until cool.

ASSEMBLE THE POPS Insert sticks into the pop maker molds and pour the basic cheesecake layer 1/4 of the way up the mold (using about 1 Tbsp per pop); wait 1 minute and then pour the chocolate cheesecake layer until you reach halfway up the mold (using about 1 Tbsp per pop). Repeat layering (waiting 1 minute in between adding each layer) until you reach the fill line. Let freeze completely, then remove pops with the Super Tool and enjoy! Repeat with remaining pops. Yields 6.

You are getting **hungry...**

very, very,
huuungry...

for
POPS!

Chocolate Coconut Cookie Mayhem

This pop is inspired by a favorite Girl Scout Cookie: the Samoa®. Be generous with the coconut and chopped wafers because you'll want some in every bite! Assembly is easier if you fill one mold at a time instead of filling all three at once.

COCONUT BASE

- 1 cup (8 oz) coconut milk (not lite)
- 1/3 cup vanilla pudding
- 2 1/2 Tbsp 2% milk
- 3 1/2 Tbsp brown sugar

EXTRAS

- 1/2 cup shredded sweetened coconut
- 18 mini vanilla wafer cookies (3/4 oz), broken into pieces
- 1 recipe Chocolate Quick Shell, p. 29

TOAST COCONUT Preheat oven to 400°F. Spread coconut in a single layer on a baking sheet lined with parchment. Bake for 10–12 minutes, checking and stirring every few minutes to prevent burning. Remove from oven and let cool completely.

MAKE THE COCONUT BASE Whisk together the coconut base ingredients until sugar has dissolved.

ASSEMBLE POPS Insert sticks into the pop maker molds and pour a drop of the coconut base (about 1/2 Tbsp per pop). Add a generous pinch of coconut and half a wafer on each side of the sticks, pushing down with a chopstick, if necessary. Repeat until you reach the fill line, topping the filled molds with a pinch of toasted coconut to create a skirt (see p. 13). You should be using a little over 1 Tbsp coconut flakes and 2–3 wafers per pop. Let freeze completely, then remove pops with the Super Tool. Repeat with remaining pops.

APPLY THE QUICK SHELL Hold a pop flat side facing up and use a small spoon to drizzle stripes crosswise onto the pop. Wait a few seconds for the shell to harden and do the same to the other side. Then dip the pop into the shell lengthwise; wait a few seconds for the shell to harden completely and enjoy! Repeat with remaining pops. Yields 6.

From left to right:
The Banana Stand, p. 88, **Nutty Chocolate Pretzel, That's a S'more** p. 83, **& Oh, Fudge!** p. 82

Coco Loco Quick Pops™

Oh, Fudge!

Catch your tastebuds by surprise with this decadent chocolate pop. We've created three fun versions of it, including Nutty Chocolate Pretzel and That's a S'more (opposite page) and The Banana Stand (p. 88).

FUDGE BASE
- 1 cup (8 oz) water
- 2 1/2 oz bittersweet chocolate
- 1/3 cup sugar
- 1 pinch salt
- 1/3 cup (2 1/2 oz) 2% milk
- 1 Tbsp half & half

MAKE THE FUDGE BASE In a medium saucepan over low heat, whisk together the water, chocolate, sugar, and salt until the chocolate has completely melted (do not boil) and chocolate granules have dissolved, about 5 minutes (test by dipping a clean spoon into the mixture; if you don't see many chocolate specks, it's ready to come off the heat). Let cool slightly (about 10 minutes). Whisk in the milk and half & half. Refrigerate until cool.

ASSEMBLE THE POPS Insert sticks into the pop maker molds and pour the cooled chocolate base until you reach the fill line. Let freeze completely, then remove pops with the Super Tool and enjoy! Repeat with remaining pops. Yields 6.

Nutty Chocolate Pretzel

Sweet, salty, crunchy, and nutty– this crazy chocolate pop has it all! Photo, p. 80.

INGREDIENTS

- 12 mini chocolate-covered pretzels
- 1 recipe Oh, Fudge!, p. 82
- 12 lightly–salted peanuts, split into halves
- 1/2 cup finely chopped, lightly–salted peanuts
- 1 recipe Chocolate Quick Shell, p. 29

ASSEMBLE THE POPS Add 1 or 2 mini chocolate-covered pretzels to the pop maker mold and insert the stick to secure them in place. Repeat with remaining molds. Pour the cooled chocolate base into the prepared molds, pausing to drop in peanut halves (4 per pop), until you reach the fill line. Let freeze completely, then remove pops with the Super Tool. Repeat with remaining pops.

Hold the pop flat side facing up and sprinkle the chopped peanuts on top of it. Use a small spoon to drizzle the Chocolate Quick Shell over the pop and wait a few seconds until the shell hardens so that the nuts are held in place. Shake off the excess nuts and enjoy! Repeat with remaining pops. Yields 6.

That's a S'more

When the moon hits your eye like a big chocolate pie, That's a S'more! Prepare to fall in love with this pop inspired by the classic combo of graham crackers, chocolate and gooey marshmallows. Photo, p. 80.

INGREDIENTS

- 1 recipe Oh, Fudge!, p. 82
- 30 mini marshmallows
- 1/4 cup crumbled graham crackers
- 1 recipe White Chocolate Quick Shell, p. 29

ASSEMBLE THE POPS Insert sticks into the pop maker molds and pour the cooled chocolate base 1/4 of the way up the molds (using about 1 Tbsp per pop). Add 1 or 2 marshmallows to each side of the sticks, pushing down with a chopstick if necessary and let freeze completely. Add crumbled graham crackers to each mold (using about 1 tsp per pop); pack down with the blunt end of a chopstick to create a dense layer. Repeat layering as desired until you reach the fill line. Let freeze completely, then remove pops with the Super Tool. Dip pops halfway into the White Chocolate Quick Shell; wait a few seconds for the shell to harden completely and enjoy! Repeat with remaining pops. Yields 6.

Askinosie Chocolate® Brownie

Askinosie is one of very few American small-batch chocolate makers that makes chocolate from scratch, straight from the bean. Their incredibly smooth, high-quality chocolate yields a rich, luscious pop. We created this pop as a celebration of our friendship with them and as a tribute to their truly amazing chocolate.

CHOCOLATE BASE

- $3/4$ cup (6 oz) water
- 2 oz Askinosie Del Tambo 70% Dark Chocolate*, chopped
- 3 Tbsp sugar
- 3 $1/2$ Tbsp 2% milk
- 1 Tbsp + $1/2$ tsp sweetened condensed milk
- 1 $1/2$ tsp water

EXTRAS

- 4 oz Askinosie Del Tambo 70% Dark Chocolate*, chopped
- $1/3$ cup (2 $1/2$ oz) coconut oil
- $1/2$ cup coarsely chopped pistachios, toasted (toasting instructions, p. 72)
- 1 fudge brownie, chopped into 24 (1" x $1/4$" x $1/4$") pieces

MAKE THE CHOCOLATE BASE In a small saucepan over very low heat, whisk together the $3/4$ cup water, 2 oz chocolate and sugar until the chocolate has completely melted (do not boil) and chocolate granules have dissolved, about 5 minutes (test by dipping a clean spoon into the mixture; if you don't see many chocolate specks, it's ready to come off the heat). Let cool

slightly (about 10 min.). Whisk in the 2% milk, condensed milk, and 1 $1/2$ tsp water. Refrigerate until cool, whisking occasionally to prevent a skin from forming.

MAKE THE QUICK SHELL Follow instructions for Chocolate Quick Shell (p. 29) using Askinosie Del Tambo 70% Dark Chocolate*.

ASSEMBLE THE POPS Insert sticks into the pop maker molds and pour the chocolate base, pausing to add pistachios and brownie pieces on each side of the sticks until you reach the fill line. Let freeze completely, then remove pops with the Super Tool. Repeat with remaining pops.

DECORATE THE POPS Dip pops into the Chocolate Quick Shell and immediately sprinkle with pistachios. Wait a few seconds for the shell to harden completely and enjoy! Repeat with remaining pops. Yields 6.

---

* Askinosie Chocolate can be purchased at askinosie.com. If you can't get your hands on Askinosie Chocolate, other fine dark chocolate can be substituted.

COCO LOCO

CPB (Chocolate Peanut Butter)

Chocolate is super. Peanut butter is awesome. Chocolate + peanut butter is super awesome! Kristina takes her chocolate and peanut butter pretty seriously and worked hard to come up with a pop that lives up to her love for this classic combination. For more chocolate & peanut butter recipes, visit Kristina's blog, The Chocolate Peanut Butter Gallery at cpbgallery.com.

CHOCOLATE LAYER
- $1/2$ cup (4 oz) water
- 3 Tbsp sugar
- 1 level Tbsp smooth peanut butter
- 1 oz bittersweet chocolate
- Pinch salt
- 3 Tbsp 2% milk
- 1 tsp water
- $1/8$ tsp white wine vinegar

PEANUT BUTTER LAYER
- $1/2$ cup (4 oz) water
- $1/4$ cup sugar
- 3 level Tbsp smooth peanut butter
- Pinch salt
- 3 Tbsp 2% milk
- $1 1/2$ tsp water
- $1/2$ tsp white wine vinegar

Pop Tip
For extra CPB, add in chopped pieces of your favorite chocolate peanut butter candy bars.

MAKE THE CHOCOLATE LAYER In a small saucepan over very low heat, whisk together the water, sugar, peanut butter, chocolate, and salt until the chocolate has completely melted (do not boil) and chocolate granules have dissolved, about 5 minutes (test by dipping a clean spoon into the mixture; if you don't see many chocolate specks, it's ready to come off the heat; peanut butter specks will remain). Let cool slightly (about 10 min.), whisking occasionally to prevent a skin from forming. Whisk in the milk, 1 tsp water, and vinegar. Refrigerate until cool.

MAKE THE PEANUT BUTTER LAYER In a small saucepan over very low heat, whisk together the $1/2$ cup water, sugar, peanut butter and salt until the mixture is warm and bubbles appear on the edge. The moment it starts to boil, remove from heat and let cool slightly (about 10 min.), whisking occasionally to prevent a skin from forming. Whisk in the milk, $1 1/2$ tsp water and vinegar. Refrigerate until cool. *(cont.)*

ASSEMBLE THE POPS Insert sticks into the pop maker molds and pour the cooled chocolate base $1/4$ of the way up the molds (using about 1 Tbsp per pop). Let freeze completely, then pour the cooled peanut butter base halfway up the molds (using about 1 Tbsp per pop). Repeat layering once more or until you reach the fill line. Let freeze completely, then remove pops with the Super Tool and enjoy! Repeat with remaining pops. Yields 6.

PBJ (Peanut Butter and Jelly)

Just when you thought it couldn't get any better, your favorite childhood lunch has transformed into an ice pop. A layer of grape juice adds a punch of brightness that perfectly balances the rich peanut butter. Photo, p. 86.

INGREDIENTS

- 1 recipe Peanut Butter Layer, p. 87
- $3/4$ cup (6 oz) pure Concord grape juice

ASSEMBLE THE POPS Follow instructions for CPB assembly (above), replacing the chocolate layer with the grape juice. Yields 6.

The Banana Stand

Take a stand and declare your love for chocolate and bananas! Photo, p. 9 & 80.

INGREDIENTS

- 1–2 bananas, sliced $1/8$" thick
- 1 recipe Oh, Fudge!, p. 82
- 1 recipe Peanut Butter Quick Shell, p. 29 (optional)

ASSEMBLE THE POPS Using the Zoku Fruit Wand (p. 12) or tweezers, apply the banana slices to the walls of the pop maker molds. Insert sticks into the prepared molds and pour the cooled chocolate base until you reach the fill line. Let freeze completely, then remove pops with the Super Tool.

APPLY THE QUICK SHELL If desired, dip the pops in the Peanut Butter Quick Shell; wait a few seconds for the shell to harden completely and enjoy! Repeat with remaining pops. Yields 6.

Salty Milk Chocolate Butterscotch

Chocolate lovers are definitely divided into two camps: dark and milk chocolate. For any in the latter, this one's for you! The salt balances out this otherwise sweet pop.

INGREDIENTS

- $3/4$ cup (6 oz) water
- 2 oz milk chocolate, chopped
- 1 $1/2$ oz butterscotch chips (just under $1/4$ cup)
- $1/2$ cup + 1 Tbsp (4 $1/2$ oz) half & half
- $1/4$ tsp table salt

MAKE THE CHOCOLATE BUTTERSCOTCH BASE In a small saucepan over low heat, whisk together the water, chocolate, and butterscotch chips until the chocolate and butterscotch chips have just melted (do not boil). Remove from heat and let cool slightly (about 10 min.). Whisk in the half & half and salt. Refrigerate until cool, whisking occasionally to prevent a skin from forming.

ASSEMBLE THE POPS Insert sticks into the pop maker molds and pour the cooled chocolate butterscotch base until you reach the fill line. Let freeze completely, then remove pops with the Super Tool and enjoy! Repeat with remaining pops. Yields 6.

Malted Milk Ball

You'll have to reserve this cinematic treat for your home theatre. Make way, popcorn— there's a new snack in town!

MALT BASE

- 3/4 cup (6 oz) whole milk
- 4 oz vanilla pudding
  (1 individual serving cup)
- 1/3 cup (2 1/2 oz) heavy cream
- 1/3 cup Ovaltine® Classic Malt Mix
- 1 1/2 tsp agave nectar

EXTRAS

- 12 large malted milk balls, sliced or chopped into pieces

MAKE THE MALT BASE Whisk together the malt base ingredients.

ASSEMBLE POPS Insert sticks into the pop maker molds and pour the malt base, pausing to add pieces of chopped malted milk balls as you pour, until you reach the fill line. Let freeze completely, then remove pops with the Super Tool and enjoy! Repeat with remaining pops. Yields 6.

Pop Tip

If you want to apply slices of malted milk balls to the walls of the Pop Maker molds, brush them with honey so they stick securely before inserting sticks and pouring pop base.

Index

ETC.

93

Conversion Charts

Volume

US	UK
1/4 tsp	1.25 ml
1/2 tsp	2.5 ml
1 tsp	5 ml
1 Tbsp / 3 tsp	15 ml
1 fl oz / 2 Tbsp	30 ml
1/4 cup	60 ml
1/3 cup	80 ml
1/2 cup	120 ml
1 cup	240 ml
1 pint / 2 cups	475 ml
1 quart / 4 cups	950 ml
1 gallon / 4 quarts	3.8 liters

Length

INCHES	CENTIMETERS
1/4	0.6
1/2	1.3
1	2.5
2	5.1
3	7.6
4	10.2
5	12.7
6	15.2
7	17.8
8	20.3
9	22.9
10	25.4
11	27.9
12	30.5

Oven Temperature

FAHRENHEIT	CELSIUS	UK GAS MARKS
200	95	–
250	120	1/2
275	135	1
300	150	2
325	165	3
350	175	4
375	190	5
400	200	6
450	230	8
500	260	10

Weight

US	METRIC
1 oz	28 g
4 oz (1/4 lb)	113 g
8 oz (1/2 lb)	227 g
12 oz (3/4 lb)	340 g
16 oz (1 lb)	454 g